THERE'S A MONSTER
IN MY CLOSET

WRITTEN BY
LILIE MANNING

ILLUSTRATED BY
NAHIDA AKTER

THERE'S A MONSTER IN MY CLOSET
AND I'M FRIGHTENED AS I CAN BE
THAT BIG BAD MONSTER IN MY CLOSET
APPEARS AT NIGHT AND HE'S SO SCARY

I PULL MY BLANKET UP REALLY HIGH
SO THAT IT COVERS UP MY HEAD
THE MONSTER THAT WAS IN MY CLOSET
IS NOW HIDING UNDERNEATH MY BED

I SCREAM SO LOUD CALLING MOM AND DAD
THAT THEY HURRY TO MY ROOM IN FEAR
BUT EVERY TIME THEY TURN THE LIGHT ON,
THAT MONSTER WILL JUST DISAPPEAR

HE LIKES TO STAY IN MY CLOSET
WHERE HE FINDS A PLACE TO HIDE
THEN AT NIGHT HE COMES OUT AND
SCARES ME WITH BIG GREEN AND YELLOW EYES

WHEN I SLEEP WITH MOM AND DAD
THERE'S NO MONSTER TO BE FOUND BUT
IN MY ROOM WHEN MY PARENTS
TURN OUT THE LIGHT HE BEGINS
TO MOVE AROUND

MY MOM TOLD ME TO DRAW A PICTURE
OF THIS MONSTER THAT I SEE SO I DREW
A PICTURE THAT LOOKED JUST LIKE HIM
AND HELD IT OUT IN FRONT OF ME

MOM LOOKED AT THE PICTURE OF THE MONSTER AND THEN HANDED IT TO DAD THEY MUST HAVE SEEN SOMETHING FUNNY BECAUSE THEY BOTH BEGAN TO LAUGH

I LOOKED AGAIN AT WHAT I DREW
TO SEE WHAT MADE THEM LAUGH
LIKE THAT BUT ALL I SAW WAS THAT
SCARY MONSTER AND NOTHING AT ALL
THAT WOULD MAKE ME LAUGH

I STARTED TO CRY BECAUSE THEY LAUGHED AT SOMETHING THAT FRIGHTENED ME THAT SCARY MONSTER WAS NOT AT ALL FUNNY. MOM AND DAD JUST COULD NOT SEE

MOM STOPPED LAUGHING ABOUT MY MONSTER WHEN SHE LOOKED AND SAW ME CRY. YOU MADE THAT MONSTER SHE SAID TO ME, AND GAVE HIM THOSE GREEN AND YELLOW EYES

SHE WENT INTO MY CLOSET AND
CAME OUT WITH A BIG BALLOON OF MINE
I LOOKED AT WHAT I THOUGHT WAS
A MONSTER AND LAUGHED SO LOUD
MYSELF THIS TIME

THAT BIG BALLOON I PAINTED EYES ON
I RAN AND PLAYED WITH IT A LOT
BUT AT NIGHT WHEN IT WAS TIME FOR BED
THAT BIG BALLOON I FORGOT ABOUT

I'M NO LONGER SCARED OF MONSTERS.
I KNOW NOW THAT THEY ARE MAKE-BELIEVE
THERE IS NOTHING HIDING INSIDE MY CLOSET,
ONLY THINGS PUT IN THERE BY ME